This
Wonderfully Wild
book belongs to:

_____

FOREWORD

Dan O'Neill
Wildlife filmmaker,
explorer and field biologist

'Some of my earliest memories are the stories my parents read to me before bed. Stories about jungles, oceans, plains and skies, and all the life within them. I believe it is those early memories that sparked my dreams of who I hoped to become, and the things I would care about – and fight for – most in the world.

This wonderful book introduces some of the most spectacular and ingenious creatures that many people don't even know exist. I'm sure these pages will ignite future protectors of snow leopards, pangolins, sifakas, and okapis, and all the lesser-known, threatened species that need all the help they can get.'

MIX
Paper from
responsible sources
FSC® C021017

ISBN: 978-1-913339-31-9
Text copyright © Loll Kirby 2021
Illustrations copyright © Ashlee Spink 2021

ADORABLE ANIMALS

WITH AMAZING ABILITIES!

Loll
Kirby

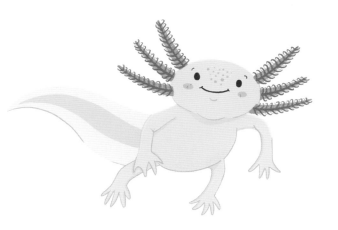

Ashlee
Spink

Published by Owlet Press, November 2021
Printed in the United Kingdom

WWW.OWLETPRESS.COM

The Okapi

Where in the world it lives: Democratic Republic of Congo in Central Africa

Habitat: rainforests

Diet: leaves, grasses, fruit and fungi

Size: up to 2.5m long and up to 350kg in weight

Okapis have brilliant night vision!

Okapis have stripy legs like zebras - this is good camouflage because it looks like sunlight shining through leaves.

They have a long, black tongue to reach for tricky buds and leaves (and it's useful for grooming as well).

Male okapis have little horns but females have knobbly bumps instead.

They eat over 100 species of plants, so they're definitely not picky eaters.

Red pandas often look like they're waddling when walking on the ground, because their front legs are shorter than their back legs.

They communicate by twittering, tweeting and whistling.

Red pandas have stripy tails that are good for camouflage and also for helping them to balance.

The Red Panda

Where in the world it lives: the Himalayas and Southwest China
Habitat: forests
Diet: mainly bamboo, but also eggs, birds and insects
Size: up to 120cm (including tail) and up to 6.2kg in weight

They are amazing acrobats who can climb up high into the trees and then clamber headfirst back down again.

They have special thumb-bones in their wrists for extra grip and they can turn their ankles backwards!

The Platypus

Where in the world it lives: Eastern Australia
Habitat: lakes, rivers and riverbanks
Diet: worms, shrimps and crayfish
Size: up to 50cm long (including tail)
and up to 2.4kg in weight

Platypuses catch their food underwater, then store it in special cheek-pouches so they can bring it to the surface before eating it.

They have biofluorescent fur, which means they glow bluish-green under black light!

On land, platypuses walk on their knuckles because this protects their delicate webbed feet.

A baby platypus is called a puggle.

Platypuses have a beak like a duck, a tail like a beaver and feet like an otter.

Snow leopards can walk in snow up to a metre deep, but they often use tracks left by other animals to save time.

Snow leopards wrap their tails around their faces like a blanket to help stay warm while they sleep!

They can't roar, so they communicate by grunting, meowing and purring.

The Snow Leopard

Where in the world it lives: Central and South Asia
Habitat: mountains
Diet: sheep, goats, smaller mammals, grass and twigs
Size: up to 2.5m long (including tail) and up to 55kg

Coatis like to rub themselves against trees and although it's not clear why, it might be because the tree's resin acts like an insect repellent.

They are very noisy eaters.

Coatis like to sleep in trees and build themselves comfortable nests from sticks and leaves.

The top of a coati's tail can
move a little bit on its own!

The Coati

Where in the world it lives: South America,
Central America, and the south-west
region of North America
Habitat: forests, semi-deserts,
mountains and grassland
Diet: lizards, invertebrates and fruit
Size: up to 69cm long (including tail)
and up to 8kg in weight

They hold their tails up straight and tall
when moving through vegetation, so that
they can spot each other easily and
stay together as a group.

Manatees are also known as sea cows!

Their tail and flippers are shaped like paddles to help them swim.

The Manatee

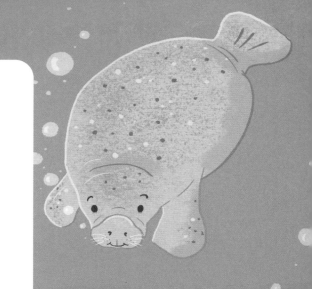

Where in the world it lives: Caribbean Sea, Gulf of Mexico, Amazon Basin and West Africa
Habitat: shallow coastal and river areas
Diet: freshwater and saltwater plants
Size: up to 4m long and up to 590kg in weight

Manatees spend half of every day submerged underwater, but they need to come up for air, every 20 minutes or so.

Their large, flexible upper lip is useful for both eating and communicating.

Although they live in water, a manatee's closest living relative is the elephant.

Male orchid mantises are less than half the size of females.

They are able to change colour slowly to blend in with their surroundings.

The Orchid Mantis

Where in the world it lives: India
and Southeast Asia
Habitat: rainforests
Diet: fruit flies, beetles and bees
Size: up to 7cm long and 30g in weight

They don't need to go and hunt for food
because they disguise themselves as flowers
and wait for the food to come to them. Their
legs look like orchid petals and they even
pretend to sway in the breeze!

Once an insect has landed
near them, they balance on
their back legs and use their
front legs to grab it.

Orchid mantises are
black and bright orange
when they're born and
only turn white as they
reach adulthood.

All baby tapirs have spots and stripes, but these markings gradually change as they grow up.

Tapirs are fast runners even though their big bodies don't seem designed for the job.

The Tapir

Where in the world it lives: South America, Central America and Southeast Asia
Habitat: forests
Diet: fruits, berries and leaves
Size: up to 2m long and up to 300kg in weight

They have very thick skin on their necks to protect them from predators.

Tapirs might live in dry forests but they like swimming in rivers. They are also able to sink down and walk along the riverbed!

They like to wallow in mud pits when the weather is hot and the mud also helps them get rid of small insects that bother them.

Some species can dive into water that's nearly 2,000 metres deep.

Other species of seal have very good long-term memories.

Some species of seal even sing to each other in the same way that birds and whales do, varying their tunes depending on whether they're underwater or on land!

Seals can migrate huge distances around the world, spending months out at sea.

The noises seals make are so expressive and distinct that scientists can tell where in the world they're from, just by listening in.

The Seal

Where in the world it lives: in all seven continents
Habitat: generally colder water around the polar and sub-polar regions
Diet: mainly fish
Size: up to 5m long and 19kg in weight (even up to 3,200kg in weight for the biggest species)

Sifakas stay perfectly upright when jumping and can leap up to 10 metres between trees as they travel through the forest. On the ground, they move by hopping sideways.

When they're not moving, they like to sunbathe high up on the branches of the trees.

They are experts at grooming and have a special toilet claw! Some of their teeth can be used as a comb.

The Sifaka

Where in the world it lives: Madagascar
Habitat: forests
Diet: leaves, flowers and fruit
Size: up to 110cm (including tail) and up to 6kg in weight

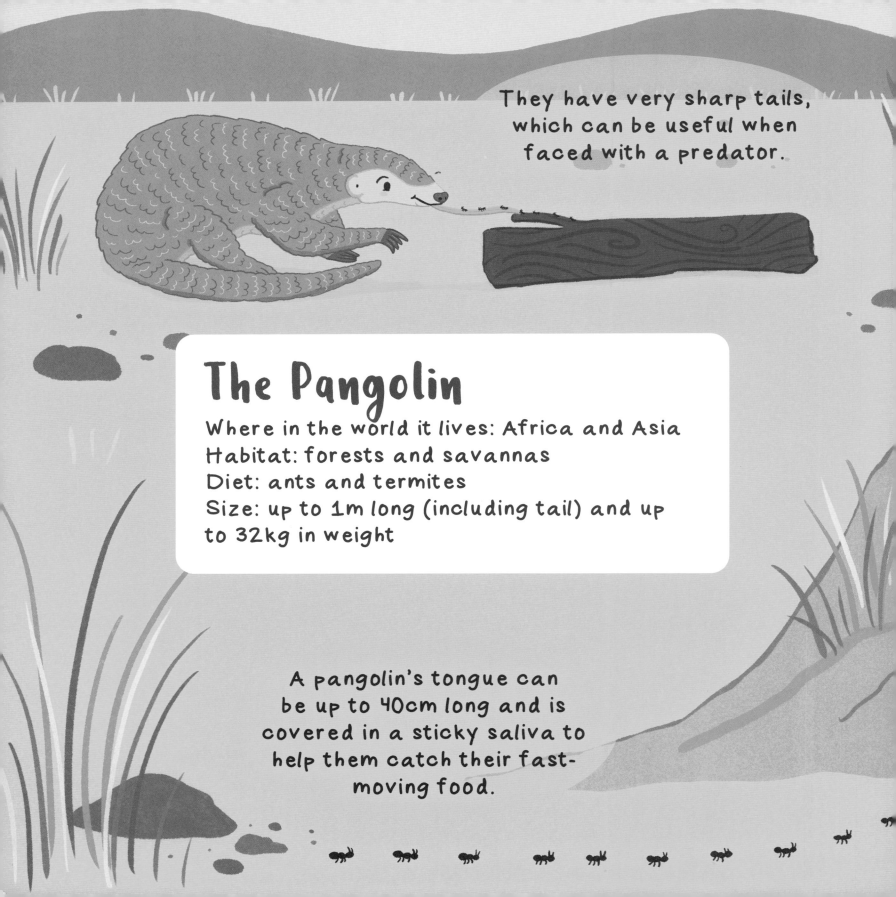

They have very sharp tails, which can be useful when faced with a predator.

The Pangolin

Where in the world it lives: Africa and Asia
Habitat: forests and savannas
Diet: ants and termites
Size: up to 1m long (including tail) and up to 32kg in weight

A pangolin's tongue can be up to 40cm long and is covered in a sticky saliva to help them catch their fast-moving food.

Pangolins are covered in up to a thousand small scales which are made from keratin (just like our fingernails).

When baby pangolins are little, they cling on to their mother's tail to stay close to her as she moves around.

Some pangolins roll themselves up into a tight ball when they're frightened, tucking their face under their tail so that they look a bit like a pine cone. They also roll themselves up to go to sleep.

Axolotls come in various colours, such as white, pink, and black.

Unlike other amphibians, they don't go through metamorphosis.

The Axolotl

Where in the world it lives: Lake Xochimilco in Mexico
Habitat: lake
Diet: crustaceans, molluscs and worms
Size: up to 45cm long and up to 300g in weight

Axolotls are also known as 'walking fish', but they're actually amphibians rather than fish.

They feed by sucking up their food.

Axolotls can grow back parts of their bodies that get damaged, including some smaller parts of the brain. Sometimes they repair the broken limb and grow a new one as well, so they end up with a spare!

You might like to use research to find out more about your favourite animals. Perhaps you could sponsor an animal or support charities that help protect our planet's precious habitats.